AN INQUIRY EARTH SCIENCE PROGRAM

INVESTIGATING SOIL

Michael J. Smith Ph.D.

John B. Southard Ph.D.

Colin Mably

Sponsored by the American Geological Institute
Supported by the National Science Foundation and
the American Geological Institute Foundation

Published by
It's About Time Inc., Armonk, NY

It's About Time, Inc.
84 Business Park Drive, Armonk, NY 10504
Phone (914) 273-2233 Fax (914) 273-2227
Toll Free (888) 698-TIME
www.Its-About-Time.com

Publisher
Laurie Kreindler

Project Editor	**Creative Artwork**	**Senior Photo Consultant**
Ruta Demery	Dennis Falcon	Bruce F. Molnia
Design	**Safety Reviewer**	**Photo Research**
John Nordland	Edward Robeck	Eric Shih
Studio Manager	**Production**	**Associate Editor**
Joan Lee	Burmar Technical Corporation	Al Mari

Technical Art
Stuart Armstrong

Illustrations and Photos
Sx (top right), S15, S39, source U.S. Department of Agriculture
Sx (top left, bottom right), Sxi, S1, S3, S4, S6, S10, S12, S24, S26, S32, S33, S35, S40 (bottom), S42, Photo disk
Sx (bottom left), S10, photos by Scott Bauer, Agricultural Research Service, USDA
Sv, Sxi, S2, S7, S16, S20, S27, S44, illustrations by Dennis Falcon
S13, S18, S19, S27, S28, S29, S30, S36, S37, S45, illustrations by Burmar Technical Corporation
S17, courtesy of the Spokane County Soil Survey Team
S23, S24, map source U.S. Geological Survey
S31, S46, photos by Eric Shih, American Geological Institute
S12, source G. Mathieson Federal Emergency Management Agency News Photo
S40 (top), photo by Jack Dykinga, Agricultural Research Service, USDA

All student activities in this textbook have been designed to be as safe as possible, and have been reviewed by professionals specifically for that purpose. As well, appropriate warnings concerning potential safety hazards are included where applicable to particular activities. However, responsibility for safety remains with the student, the classroom teacher, the school principals, and the school board.

Investigating Earth Systems™ is a registered trademark of the American Geological Institute. Registered names and trademarks, etc. used in this publication, even without specific indication thereof, are not to be considered unprotected by law.

It's About Time™ is a registered trademark of It's About Time, Inc. Registered names and trademarks, etc. used in this publication, even without specific indication thereof, are not to be considered unprotected by law.

© Copyright 2001: American Geological Institute

All right reserved. No part of this publication may be reproduced, stored in a retrieval system, or transmitted, in any form or by any means, electronic, mechanical, photocopying, recording, or otherwise, without the prior written permission of the copyright owner.

Care has been taken to trace the ownership of copyright material contained in this publication. The publisher will gladly receive any information that will rectify any reference or credit line in subsequent editions.

Printed and bound in the United States of America

ISBN #1-58591-073-2

1 2 3 4 5 QC 04 03 02 01 00

This project was supported, in part, by the
National Science Foundation (grant no. 9353035)

Opinions expressed are those of the authors and not necessarily those of the National Science Foundation or the donors of the American Geological Institute Foundation.

Acknowledgements

Principal Investigator

Michael Smith is Director of Education at the American Geological Institute in Alexandria, Virginia. Dr. Smith worked as an exploration geologist and hydrogeologist. He began his earth science teaching career with Shady Side Academy in Pittsburgh, PA in 1988 and most recently taught Earth Science at the Charter School of Wilmington, DE. He earned a doctorate from the University of Pittsburgh's Cognitive Studies in Education Program and joined the faculty of the University of Delaware School of Education in 1995. Dr. Smith received the Outstanding Earth Science Teacher Award for Pennsylvania from the National Association of Geoscience Teachers in 1991, served as Secretary of the National Earth Science Teachers Association, and is a reviewer for Science Education and The Journal of Research in Science Teaching. He worked on the Delaware Teacher Standards, Delaware Science Assessment, National Board of Teacher Certification, and AAAS Project 2061 Curriculum Evaluation programs.

Senior Writer

Dr. Southard received his undergraduate degree from the Massachusetts Institute of Technology in 1960 and his doctorate in geology from Harvard University in 1966. After a National Science Foundation postdoctoral fellowship at the California Institute of Technology, he joined the faculty at the Massachusetts Institute of Technology, where he is currently Professor of Geology. He was awarded the MIT School of Science teaching prize in 1989 and was one of the first cohort of first MacVicar Fellows at MIT, in recognition of excellence in undergraduate teaching. He has taught numerous undergraduate courses in introductory geology, sedimentary geology, field geology, and environmental earth science both at MIT and in Harvard's adult education program. He was editor of the Journal of Sedimentary Petrology from 1992 to 1996, and he continues to do technical editing of scientific books and papers for SEPM, a professional society for sedimentary geology.

Project Director/Curriculum Designer

Colin Mably has been a key curriculum developer for several NSF-supported national curriculum projects. As learning materials designer to the American Geological Institute, he has directed the design and development of the IES curriculum modules and also training workshops for pilot and field-test teachers.

INVESTIGATING SOIL

Project Team

Marcus Milling
Executive Director - AGI, VA

Michael Smith
Principal Investigator - Director of Education - AGI, VA

Colin Mably
Project Director/Curriculum Designer - Educational Visions, MD

Fred Finley
Project Evaluator - University of Minnesota, MN

Lynn Lindow
Pilot Test Evaluator - University of Minnesota, MN

Harvey Rosenbaum
Field Test Evaluator - Montgomery School District, MD

Ann Benbow
Project Advisor - American Chemical Society, DC

Robert Ridky
Original Project Director - University of Maryland, MD

Chip Groat
Original Principal Investigator - University of Texas - El Paso, TX

Marilyn Suiter
Original Co-principal Investigator - AGI, VA

William Houston
Project Manager

Eric Shih
Project Assistant

Original Writers

George Dawson
Florida State University, FL

Joe Donoghue
Florida State University, FL

Robert Gastaldo
Auburn University, AL

Colin Mably
Educational Visions, MD

Laurie Martin-Vermilyea
American Geological Institute

Mike Mogil
How The Weather Works, MD

Mary Poulton
University of Arizona, AZ

Robert Ridky
University of Maryland, MD

Michael Smith
American Geological Institute, VA

Advisory Board

Jane Crowder
Middle School Teacher, WA

Kerry Davidson
Louisiana Board of Regents, LA

Joseph D. Exline
Educational Consultant, VA

Louis A. Fernandez
California State University, CA

Frank Watt Ireton
National Earth Science Teachers Association, DC

LeRoy Lee
Wisconsin Academy of Sciences, Arts and Letters, WI

Donald W. Lewis
Chevron Corporation, CA

James V. O'Connor (deceased)
University of the District of Columbia, DC

Roger A. Pielke Sr.
Colorado State University, CO

Dorothy Stout
Cypress College, CA

Lois Veath
Advisory Board Chairperson - Chadron State College, NE

Pilot Test Teachers

Debbie Bambino - Philadelphia, PA
Barbara Barden - Rittman, OH
Louisa Bliss - Bethlehem, NH
Mike Bradshaw - Houston TX
Greta Branch - Reno, NV
Garnetta Chain - Piscataway, NJ
Roy Chambers Portland, OR
Laurie Corbett - Sayre, PA
James Cole - New York, NY
Collette Craig - Reno, NV
Anne Douglas - Houston, TX
Jacqueline Dubin - Roslyn, PA
Jane Evans - Media, PA
Gail Gant - Houston, TX
Joan Gentry - Houston, TX
Pat Gram - Aurora, OH
Robert Haffner - Akron, OH
Joe Hampel - Swarthmore, PA
Wayne Hayes - West Green, GA
Mark Johnson - Reno, NV
Cheryl Joloza - Philadelphia, PA
Jeff Luckey - Houston, TX
Karen Luniewski - Reistertown, MD
Cassie Major - Plainfield, VT
Carol Miller - Houston, TX
Melissa Murray - Reno, NV
Mary-Lou Northrop - North Kingstown, RI

Keith Olive - Ellensburg, WA
Tracey Oliver - Philadelphia, PA
Nicole Pfister - Londonderry, VT
Beth Price - Reno, NV
Joyce Ramig - Houston, TX
Julie Revilla - Woodbridge, VA
Steve Roberts - Meredith, NH
Cheryl Skipworth - Philadelphia, PA
Brent Stenson - Valdosta, GA
Elva Stout - Evans, GA
Regina Toscani - Philadelphia, PA
Bill Waterhouse - North Woodstock, NH
Leonard White - Philadelphia, PA
Paul Williams - Lowerford, VT
Bob Zafran - San Jose, CA
Missi Zender - Twinsburg, OH

Field Test Teachers

Eric Anderson - Carson City, NV
Katie Bauer - Rockport, ME
Kathleen Berdel - Philadelphia, PA
Wanda Blake - Macon, GA
Beverly Bowers - Mannington, WV
Rick Chiera - Monroe Falls, OH
Don Cole - Akron, OH
Patte Cotner - Bossier City, LA

Johnny DeFreese - Haughton, LA
Mary Devine - Astoria, NY
Cheryl Dodes - East Meadow, NY
Brenda Engstrom - Warwick, RI
Lisa Gioe-Cordi - Brooklyn, NY
Pat Gram - Aurora, OH
Mark Johnson - Reno, NV
Chicory Koren - Kent, OH
Marilyn Krupnick - Philadelphia, PA
Melissa Loftin - Bossier City, LA
John Longley - Peru, ME
Janet Lundy - Reno, NV
Vaughn Martin - Easton, ME
Anita Mathis - Fort Valley, GA
Laurie Newton - Truckee, NV
Debbie O'Gorman - Reno, NV
Joe Parlier - Barnesville, GA
Sunny Posey - Bossier City, LA
Beth Price - Reno, NV
Stan Robinson - Mannington, WV
Mandy Thorne - Mannington, WV
Marti Tomko - Westminster, MD
Jim Trogden - Rittman, OH
Torri Weed - Stonington, ME
Gene Winegart - Shreveport, LA
Dawn Wise - Peru, ME
Paula Wright - Gray, GA

IMPORTANT NOTICE

The *Investigating Earth Systems*™ series of modules is intended for use by students under the direct supervision of a qualified teacher. The experiments described in this book involve substances that may be harmful if they are misused or if the procedures described are not followed. Read cautions carefully and follow all directions. Do not use or combine any substances or materials not specifically called for in carrying out experiments. Other substances are mentioned for educational purposes only and should not be used by students unless the instructions specifically indicate.

The materials, safety information, and procedures contained in this book are believed to be reliable. This information and these procedures should serve only as a starting point for classroom or laboratory practices, and they do not purport to specify minimal legal standards or to represent the policy of the American Geological Institute. No warranty, guarantee, or representation is made by the American Geological Institute as to the accuracy or specificity of the information contained herein, and the American Geological Institute assumes no responsibility in connection therewith. The added safety information is intended to provide basic guidelines for safe practices. It cannot be assumed that all necessary warnings and precautionary measures are contained in the printed material and that other additional information and measures may not be required.

This work is based upon work supported by the National Science Foundation under Grant No. 9353035 with additional support from the Chevron Foundation. Any opinions, findings, and conclusions or recommendations expressed in this publication are those of the authors and do not necessarily reflect the views of the National Science Foundation or the Chevron Foundation. Any mention of trade names does not imply endorsement from the National Science Foundation or the Chevron Foundation.

Table of Contents

Introducing Soil	Sx
Why Is Soil Important?	Sxi
Investigation 1: Beginning to Investigate Soil	S1
Types of Soil	S4
Investigation 2: Separating Soil by Settling	S6
Gravity and Friction	S10
Investigation 3: Separating Soil by Sieving	S12
Materials Found in Soil	S14
Investigation 4: Examining Core Samples of Soil	S17
Topographic Maps	S23
Investigation 5: Water and Other Chemicals in Soil	S26
The Importance of Water and Other Chemicals in Soil	S32
Investigation 6: Soil Erosion	S35
Soil Erosion	S39
Investigation 7: Using Soil Data to Plan a Garden	S42
The Big Picture	S48
Glossary	S49

Investigating Earth Systems

INVESTIGATING SOIL

Using Investigating Earth Systems

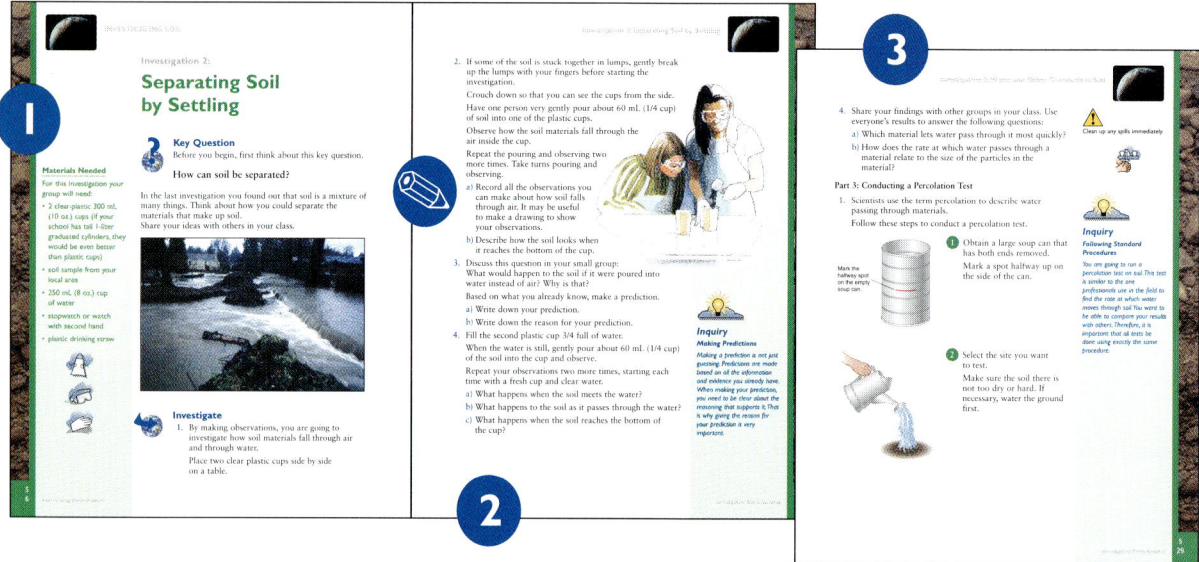

Look for the following features in this module to help you learn about the Earth system.

1. Key Question
Before you begin, you will be asked to think about the key question you will investigate. You do not need to come up with a correct answer. You are just expected to take some time to think about what you already know. You can then share your ideas with your small group and with the class.

2. Investigate
Geoscientists learn about the Earth system by doing investigations. That is exactly what you will be doing. Sometimes you will be given the procedure steps to follow. Other times you will need to decide what question you want to investigate and what procedure to follow.

3. Inquiry
You will use inquiry processes to investigate and solve problems in an orderly way. Look for these reminders about the processes you are using.

Throughout your investigations you will keep your own journal. Your journal is like one that scientists keep when they investigate a scientific question. You can enter anything you think is important during the investigation. There will also be questions after many of the **Investigate** steps for you to answer and enter in your journal. You will also need think about how the Earth works as a set of systems. You can write the connections you make after each investigation on your *Earth System Connection* sheet in your journal.

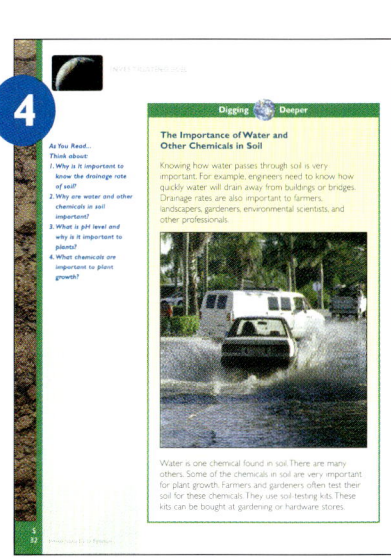
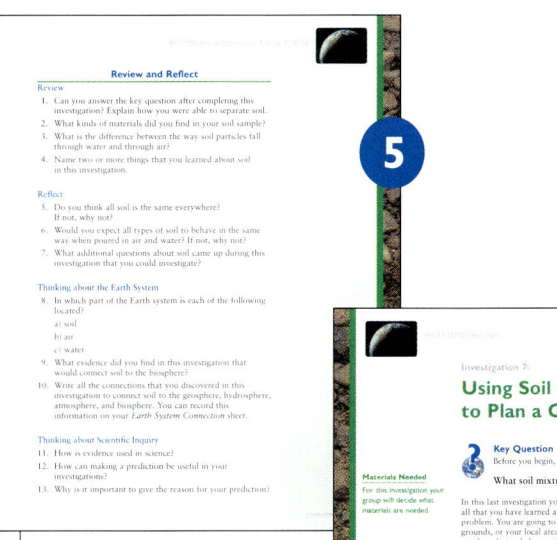

4. Digging Deeper
Scientists build on knowledge that others have discovered through investigation. In this section you can read about the insights scientists have about the question you are investigating. The questions in **As You Read** will help you focus on the information you are looking for.

5. Review and Reflect
After you have completed each investigation, you will be asked to reflect on what you have learned and how it relates to the "big picture" of the Earth system. You will also be asked to think about what scientific inquiry processes you used.

6. Investigation: Putting It All Together
In the last investigation of the module you will have a chance to "put it all together." You will be asked to apply all that you have learned in the previous investigation to solve a practical problem. This module is just the beginning! You continue to learn about the Earth system every time you ask questions and make observations about the world around you.

Investigating Earth Systems

S
vii

INVESTIGATING SOIL

The Earth System

The Earth System is a set of systems that work together in making the world we know. Four of these important systems are:

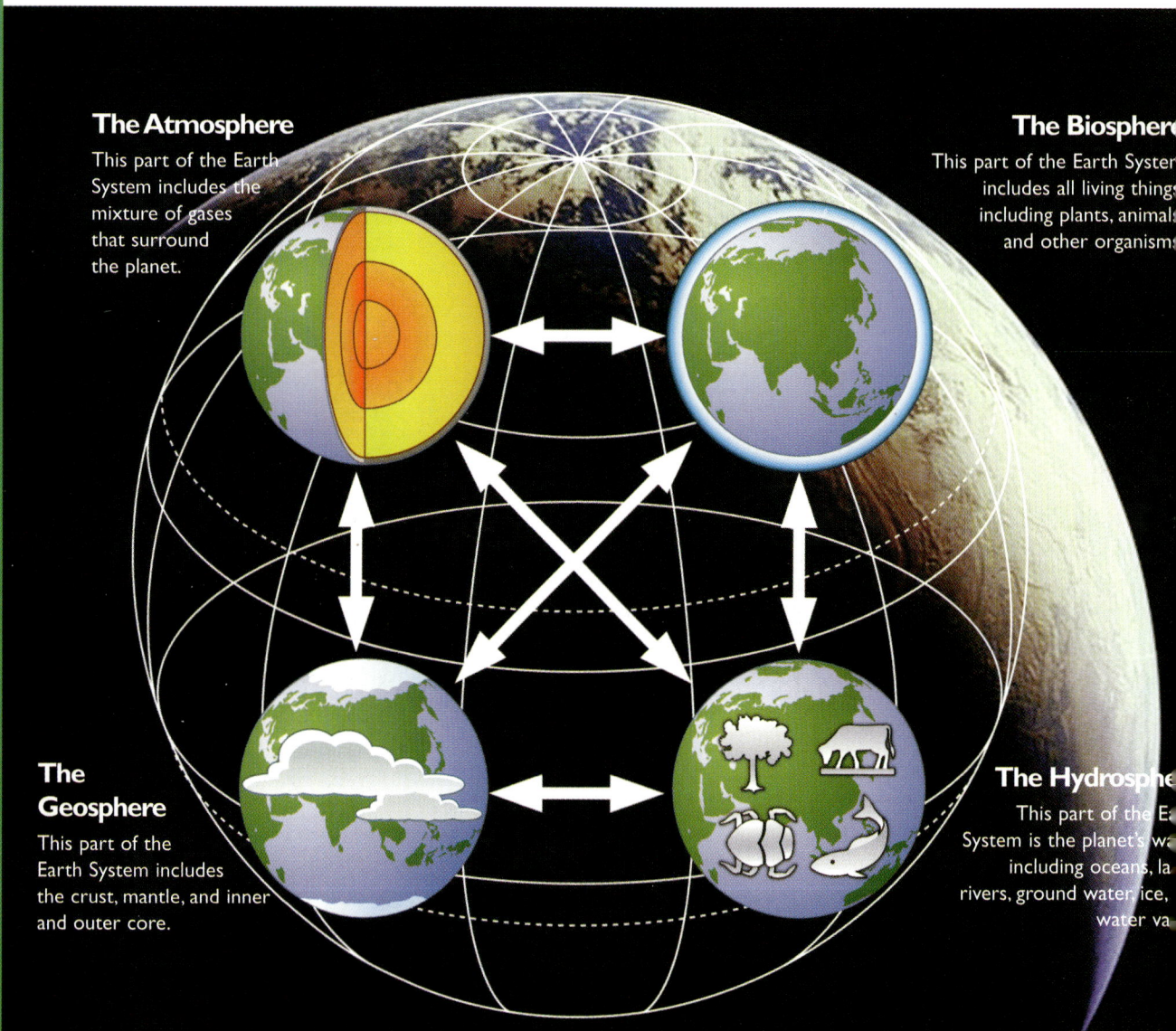

The Atmosphere
This part of the Earth System includes the mixture of gases that surround the planet.

The Biosphere
This part of the Earth System includes all living things, including plants, animals, and other organisms.

The Geosphere
This part of the Earth System includes the crust, mantle, and inner and outer core.

The Hydrosphere
This part of the Earth System is the planet's water, including oceans, lakes, rivers, ground water, ice, and water vapor.

These systems, and others, have been working together since the Earth's beginning about 4.5 billion years ago. They are still working, because the Earth is always changing, even though we cannot always observe these changes. Energy from within and outside the Earth leads to changes in the Earth System. Changes in any one of these systems affects the others. This is why we think of the Earth as made of interrelated systems.

During your investigations, keep the Earth System in mind. At the end of each investigation you will be asked to think about how the things you have discovered fit with the Earth System.

To further understand the Earth System, take a look at the illustration shown to the left.

INVESTIGATING SOIL

Introducing Soil

Did you ever wonder how soil is formed?

Have you ever seen a dust storm?

Why is there soil in the water?

Have you ever looked at things that live in the soil?

Why Is Soil Important?

Soil may be something that you have only thought of as being under your feet. Soil is much more than that. It is one of Earth's greatest natural resources. Almost all of the world's food crops grow in soil, and the world's livestock eat plants that grow in soil.

Most plants put their roots down into the soil, and many kinds of animals make their homes in soil. Most building foundations are put into the soil. The layer of soil that covers the land is very thin compared to the radius of the Earth. The depth of soil can vary widely on the Earth, from a few centimeters to tens of meters. This is not very much considering the importance of the soil layer to life on Earth!

What Will You Investigate?

To help you understand the science of soil, you will study local soil samples. You will also do research to see what types of garden plants grow best in the soil. Here are some of the characteristics of soil that you will investigate:

- the kinds of materials in soil;
- the arrangement of soil materials;
- the amount of water the soil can hold;
- how water flows through soil;
- how soil is eroded.

You will need to practice your problem-solving skills and be good observers and recorders. You will also need to be creative in finding out information about your local soil. It will be necessary for you to consult a variety of sources. To complete your investigations you will work together with other members of your class.

Investigating Earth Systems

Investigation 1: Beginning to Investigate Soil

Investigation 1:
Beginning to Investigate Soil

 **Key Question**

Before you begin, first think about this key question.

What can you investigate about soil?

Think about what you already know about soil. Write a question you could investigate about soil based on what you know. Think about what you could do with a soil sample to find an answer to your question.

Share your thinking with others in your group and with your class. Make a list that combines everyone's questions and ideas about things to do. Keep the list for later in this investigation.

Materials Needed

For this investigation your group will need:

- soil sample (from your local area)
- white paper
- hand lens
- tools for separating soil (plastic knife, tweezers, or tongue depressor)
- cup of water
- paper towels

 **Investigate**

1. Cover a large, flat workspace with white paper.

   Place a soil sample on the paper.

   Divide up the soil so that each member of your group has about a handful.

Keep the soil on the paper covering the work area.

Investigating Earth Systems

INVESTIGATING SOIL

⚠ Never place your nose over the sample and inhale. Never taste anything in a science lab. Take care not to rub soil into your eyes.

2. Use your senses of seeing, feeling, and smelling (not tasting!) to examine the soil sample. To identify the odor of the soil sample wave your hand over the sample toward your nose.

   a) Record your observations. It is important to record your observations in a way that others can see and understand. One example is shown below. You can adapt this example to suit your needs, or you can choose another method that you think would be better.

3. Use the tools to separate and examine the soil more closely.

   a) Add any new observations to your data table or diagram.

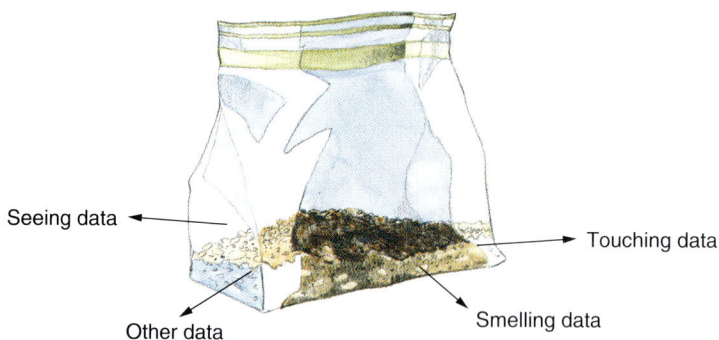

Seeing data — Touching data — Smelling data — Other data

4. Use your data to answer the following questions:

   a) Do you think all groups will have the same findings? Why or why not?

   b) Which questions about soil from your original list have your observations answered? Which questions are still unanswered?

Investigating Earth Systems

Investigation 1: Beginning to Investigate Soil

5. In your group, decide on one question to investigate further. It might be one of the unanswered questions from your original list, or a new question that has occurred to you from your work so far.

   Prepare a plan to investigate your question. You will need to design an investigation so that it:
   - will lead to an answer (or a part of an answer) to your question;
   - can be done in your working space;
   - can be done safely with the tools and time available;
   - uses a clear method of recording the results.

   a) Write down your plan for investigating your question.

6. With the approval of your teacher, conduct your investigation.

   If necessary, repeat your investigation several times to make sure of your results.

   a) Record your observations and results.

7. Present the findings of your group to the rest of the class.

   Listen to the results of other groups' investigations.

   a) Record and display the findings of all groups.
   b) As a class, what questions do you still think need to be answered?

Inquiry

Scientific Questions

Scientific inquiry starts with a question. Scientists take what they already know about a topic, then form a question to investigate further. The question and its investigation are designed to expand their understanding of the topic. You are doing the same.

Showing Your Findings to Others

One way to present your findings might be for groups to visit each other's working area and observe what each group has done. Another way is for each group to make a presentation in front of the class.

Have your plan approved by your teacher before you begin your investigation.

Clean up spills immediately.

Investigating Earth Systems

S 3

INVESTIGATING SOIL

As You Read...
Think about:
1. What are the main things found in soil?
2. How is soil formed?
3. What determines the type of soil that is formed?

Digging Deeper

Types of Soil

There are many kinds of soil. A group of soil scientists from the U.S. made up a way of grouping soils that is used around the world. This grouping has hundreds of named soil types! All soils, however, are made of just a few main components. Soil consists of fine particles of minerals and rocks, decaying plants, and living plants and animals. You can easily see the larger plants and animals. There are even more tiny plants and animals that you can only see with a microscope.

Soil forms as the solid rock of the Earth, called bedrock, breaks down. It usually takes thousands of years for soil to form from bedrock. In some places, soil forms directly on top of bedrock. In other places, soil forms on a thick layer of loose rock and mineral material. This material, called sediment, has been carried from distant areas by rivers or glaciers.

What determines the type of soil that forms? Only two things are most important: bedrock type, and climate. It should make sense to you that different kinds of bedrock make different kinds of soil. Climate is also important. Water helps chemical reactions in soil to take place. Young soils are soils which have just started to form. In young soils bedrock is more important than climate in determining the type of soil. In old soils, which have become fully formed, climate is usually more important.

Most soils are only a meter or two deep. The nature of the soil changes as you go down. When soil scientists study a soil, they look carefully at the whole thickness of the soil. This type of section of soil is called a soil profile. In a later investigation you will have a chance to study a real soil profile.

Investigation 1: Beginning to Investigate Soil

Review and Reflect

Review

1. What questions about soil were you able to answer from this investigation?
2. What questions about soil do you still want answered?

Reflect

3. What did you expect to find in soil?
4. What surprised you about soil when you looked at it closely?
5. a) What materials did you find in soil?
   b) Where do you think these materials came from?

Thinking about the Earth System

6. Write any connection that you have discovered in this investigation to connect soil to the geosphere, hydrosphere, atmosphere, and biosphere. You can record this information on your *Earth System Connection* sheet.

Thinking about Scientific Inquiry

7. In which part(s) of the investigation did you:
   a) Explore questions to answer by inquiry?
   b) Conduct an investigation?
   c) Design an investigation?
   d) Show evidence and reasons to others?
8. How did you collect and manage your data?
9. What did you do in this investigation to make sure that your results were reliable?

INVESTIGATING SOIL

Investigation 2:

Separating Soil by Settling

Key Question
Before you begin, first think about this key question.

How can soil be separated?

In the last investigation you found out that soil is a mixture of many things. Think about how you could separate the materials that make up soil.
Share your ideas with others in your class.

Materials Needed

For this investigation your group will need:

- 2 clear-plastic 300 mL (10 oz.) cups (if your school has tall 1-liter graduated cylinders, they would be even better than plastic cups)
- soil sample from your local area
- 250 mL (8 oz.) cup of water
- stopwatch or watch with second hand
- plastic drinking straw

Investigate

1. By making observations, you are going to investigate how soil materials fall through air and through water.

   Place two clear plastic cups side by side on a table.

Investigation 2: Separating Soil by Settling

2. If some of the soil is stuck together in lumps, gently break up the lumps with your fingers before starting the investigation.

   Crouch down so that you can see the cups from the side.

   Have one person very gently pour about 60 mL (1/4 cup) of soil into one of the plastic cups.

   Observe how the soil materials fall through the air inside the cup.

   Repeat the pouring and observing two more times. Take turns pouring and observing.

   a) Record all the observations you can make about how soil falls through air. It may be useful to make a drawing to show your observations.

   b) Describe how the soil looks when it reaches the bottom of the cup.

3. Discuss this question in your small group: What would happen to the soil if it were poured into water instead of air? Why is that?

   Based on what you already know, make a prediction.

   a) Write down your prediction.

   b) Write down the reason for your prediction.

4. Fill the second plastic cup 3/4 full of water.

   When the water is still, gently pour about 60 mL (1/4 cup) of the soil into the cup and observe.

   Repeat your observations two more times, starting each time with a fresh cup and clear water.

   a) What happens when the soil meets the water?

   b) What happens to the soil as it passes through the water?

   c) What happens when the soil reaches the bottom of the cup?

Inquiry
Making Predictions

Making a prediction is not just guessing. Predictions are made based on all the information and evidence you already have. When making your prediction, you need to be clear about the reasoning that supports it. That is why giving the reason for your prediction is very important.

Investigating Earth Systems

INVESTIGATING SOIL

Inquiry

The Importance of Evidence

The word **evidence** may be familiar to you in criminal investigations. However, evidence is also important in science. In science, valid conclusions depend on evidence that can be trusted. Others should be able to do the same experiment and come up with the same evidence.

5. Look at the prediction you made and the reason you gave for your prediction.

   If something different happened from what you expected, discuss what the reasons might be.

   a) How accurate was your prediction?

   b) Did anything happen that you were not expecting? If so, what?

   c) Does your reason make good sense?

   d) If necessary, rewrite your reason to include any new information or ideas you have. Base your explanation on the evidence you have.

6. Allow your water and soil mixture to settle for 5 minutes.

   Make observations every minute during this time.

   a) Record everything you observe. An example of a data table is given below. You can change it to suit your needs.

Time (minutes)	Observations
After 1	
After 2	
After 3	
After 4	
After 5	

Clean up any spills immediately.

7. Stir your soil and water mixture with the drinking straw, then let it settle.

   Observe what is happening to the soil particles in the water. Note if all particles are behaving in the same way.

   a) Record your observations.

   b) How can you explain what you observe?

Investigation 2: Separating Soil by Settling

8. In your small group, discuss what you think will happen to this mixture if you allow it to settle for a much longer time.

    Based on what you see happening now, predict what the soil inside the cup will look like in 24 hours.

    a) Write down your prediction.

    b) Write down the reason for your prediction.

9. Label your cup in a way that you can identify it among others.

    Find a safe place to store your water and soil mixture undisturbed for the next 24 hours.

10. After 24 hours examine your soil and water mixture carefully.

    Observe how it has changed.

    a) How many kinds of materials can you now observe in the soil?

    b) What do you think these are?

    c) How do you think you could find out what the different materials are?

    d) How accurate was your prediction?

11. Design a good way to show your findings to others. Share your findings with the class.

    Record your information in a way that you can add more to it later. The following shows one way to record your findings:

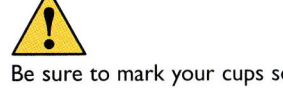

Be sure to mark your cups so others know what is in them.

| What is Found in Soil ||
Finding	Evidence
Soil is composed of many things.	We found stones, bits of...

Investigating Earth Systems

S
9

INVESTIGATING SOIL

As You Read...
Think about:
1. What makes objects fall toward the center of the Earth?
2. Why do large, heavy objects fall faster than small, light ones?

Digging Deeper

Gravity and Friction

The Earth's gravity pulls all things toward the center of the Earth. The soil materials fell to the bottom of the cup because of the pull of gravity. You know from experience that the speed of a falling object depends on the weight and the size of the object. A bowling ball falls much faster than an air-filled balloon. They are about the same size but the bowling ball is much heavier. A marble falls more slowly than a bowling ball. They are both made of the same type of material, but the bowling ball is much larger, and therefore much heavier. This probably seems very natural to you. However, it is not that simple to explain why. If you dropped those objects on the Moon, they would all fall at the same speed! The difference has to do with a force that

keeps one object from moving against another object. This force is called friction. In this investigation the friction was between the air or water and the falling particles. There is no air on the Moon, so there would be no friction to hold back falling objects.

The soil in your sample probably was made up of differently sized particles. They may have been as large as sand grains or pebbles, or as small as fine mineral particles. The larger particles tended to fall faster, so they reached the bottom of the cup first. It took a long time, however, for the dust to settle in the air and for the muddy water to become clear again. Also, it took longer for the particles to settle in water than in air. That is because the friction is greater in water than in air.

Investigating Earth Systems

Investigation 2: Separating Soil by Settling

Review and Reflect

Review

1. Can you answer the key question after completing this investigation? Explain how you were able to separate soil.
2. What kinds of materials did you find in your soil sample?
3. What is the difference between the way soil particles fall through water and through air?
4. Name two or more things that you learned about soil in this investigation.

Reflect

5. Do you think all soil is the same everywhere? If not, why not?
6. Would you expect all types of soil to behave in the same way when poured in air and water? If not, why not?
7. What additional questions about soil came up during this investigation that you could investigate?

Thinking about the Earth System

8. In which part of the Earth system is each of the following located?
    a) soil
    b) air
    c) water
9. What evidence did you find in this investigation that would connect soil to the biosphere?
10. Write all the connections that you discovered in this investigation to connect soil to the geosphere, hydrosphere, atmosphere, and biosphere. You can record this information on your *Earth System Connection* sheet.

Thinking about Scientific Inquiry

11. How is evidence used in science?
12. How can making a prediction be useful in your investigations?
13. Why is it important to give the reason for your prediction?

Investigating Earth Systems

INVESTIGATING SOIL

Investigation 3:

Separating Soil by Sieving

Key Question

Before you begin, think again about the key question from the last investigation.

How can soil be separated?

In the last investigation, you used the method of settling to separate the different materials in a soil sample. You probably also thought of other ways to separate the materials.
Share your thinking with others in your group and with your class. Make a list that combines everyone's ideas about other methods for separating soil.

Materials Needed

For this investigation your group will need:

- soil sample (from your local area)
- large piece of white poster board
- 4 squares of white poster board (about 10 cm (4") square)
- 3 large mixing bowls
- plastic strainer, with about 2-mm diameter holes
- kitchen sieve, with about 0.5-mm diameter holes
- large plastic cups
- plastic spoon
- hand lens

Investigate

1. Spread the soil sample onto a piece of poster board to dry.
   When it is completely dry, break up any lumps by pressing gently on them with your thumb.

Investigating Earth Systems

Investigation 3: Separating Soil by Sieving

2. Put the plastic strainer over one of the large bowls.

   Pour your soil sample into the strainer.

   Shake the strainer to make the finer part of the soil pass through.

   If you see any more lumps of soil in the strainer, break them up gently and shake again.

Shake the strainer gently.

3. Pour the material from the strainer into a large plastic cup.

   Fill the cup with warm water.

   Stir the water with a spoon for about 10 s.

   Skim off any floating material with the spoon, and put it on a small square of poster board to dry.

4. Stir the water again and wait two or three seconds.

   Pour the water off. Stop just before you lose the coarse material at the bottom of the cup.

   Repeat this a few times, until there is almost no fine cloudy material in the water.

   Dump or scrape the remaining material onto another small square of poster board to dry.

Label all samples that are left to dry so that others know what they are.

INVESTIGATING SOIL

Inquiry
Making Observations

Careful observations and descriptions of materials and processes are the basis for all good science. Scientists first describe what they see, as carefully as they can. Only then do they try to form theories and interpret their data.

Clean up spills immediately.

As You Read...
Think about:
1. Why is it important to have methods of separating soil samples?
2. What things are you likely to find in soil?

5. Put the kitchen sieve over the second bowl, and pour the dry soil that passed through the strainer into the sieve.

Repeat steps 3 and 4.

Combine any floating material you caught in this step with the floating material you caught earlier.

6. Now you have separated your soil sample into four parts: coarse particles, medium-sized particles, fine particles, and floating particles.

After each part has dried, examine it with the hand lens under strong light. Try to identify the materials in each part. It helps to examine the material both when it is wet and when it is dry.

It will be much harder to identify the materials in the finest part than in the coarser parts. Even soil scientists, using specialized equipment, have trouble with the very finest materials in soils.

a) Record your observations on a data sheet. Note the size of the particles, the shape of particles, the color of the particles, and what you think the particles are made of.

b) On another sheet of paper, write down detailed descriptions of each item in your data table. Describe everything about the materials you can think of. Each detail, no matter how small, might turn out to be very important when you try to interpret your observations.

Digging Deeper

Materials Found in Soil

Soil scientists separate soil using a stack of several sieves. The sieves have holes with slightly different sizes. The coarsest sieve is at the top of the stack, and the finest sieve is at the bottom. You used a similar but simpler method in this investigation. This method of separating the soil materials gives you the best chance for looking at the different kinds of materials. You can think of it as a "divide and conquer" method!

Investigation 3: Separating Soil by Sieving

Most soils contain many kinds of material. All soils consist mainly of two kinds of material: particles of minerals and rocks, and organic matter. Organic matter is any matter that is or was once living.

Your soil is likely to have several kinds of rock and mineral particles. A few kinds are very common. Many other kinds are sometimes common, but usually are not. The three most common kinds are quartz particles, feldspar particles, and small pieces of rock. Your sample is very likely to have a lot of at least one of these three kinds of particles.

Quartz particles have irregular shapes. They look gray and glassy. Their surfaces are often stained brown or orange, because they are coated with rust. Feldspar particles are usually white or cream colored. Their surfaces are often flat, at least partly, rather than irregular. There are many kinds of rock particles. You can tell them apart from the mineral particles because rocks are made of many different particles of minerals, all stuck tightly together.

The finest part of your soil is probably mostly very small flakes of clay. They are too small for you to see even with a hand lens. Sandy soils are loose and easy to dig. Soils with a lot of clay are harder to dig. Some plants prefer sandy soils, and others soils with more clay.

INVESTIGATING SOIL

Most soils have lots of organic matter. Some of the organic matter is in the form of living things. The ones you might see in your sample are large, like earthworms or insects. There are also many very tiny plants and animals, called microorganisms. There are many more of these, but you can't see them without a microscope. In a typical soil, there are millions of them in every cubic centimeter!

Most soils are also rich in decaying plants. If the plant has decayed only slightly, you can usually recognize scraps of leaves, roots, and seeds. When the plant has decayed more, it turns into a soft, fine, dark material called humus. Humus is very important in soils. New plants can easily put their roots into humus. It is also good at holding water for later use by growing plants.

Review and Reflect

Review

1. Which kinds of materials in your sample came from plants?
2. Which kinds of materials came from animals?
3. Which kinds of materials formed in the soil, and which were present before the soil began to form?
4. Which kinds of material might have dropped into the soil from the sky?

Reflect

5. Why was it important for your study of soil, to be able to separate a sample of soil?

Thinking about Scientific Inquiry

6. What type of evidence did you collect in this investigation?
7. How did the use of tools in this investigation help you answer the key question?

Investigation 4: Examining Core Samples of Soil

Investigation 4:

Examining Core Samples of Soil

Key Question

Before you begin, first think about this key question.

Is all soil the same?

You have been looking at one soil sample. Think about how this sample would compare with samples from different places. Share your ideas with others in your class.

Materials Needed

In this investigation your group will need:

- map of sampling area
- piece of 2.5 cm (1") heavy duty PVC pipe about 25 cm (10") long
- wooden block
- hammer
- garden or work glove
- piece of wooden dowel 30 cm (12") long that fits inside PVC pipe
- large sheet of white poster board or paper
- plastic wrap
- colored pencils
- plastic knife
- hand lens
- tweezers or tongue depressor

Investigate

Part 1: Collecting the Soil Samples

1. To investigate differences in soils, it is important to collect all samples using the same procedure.

   Once you have selected a site, use the procedure on the following pages to collect each sample.

INVESTIGATING SOIL

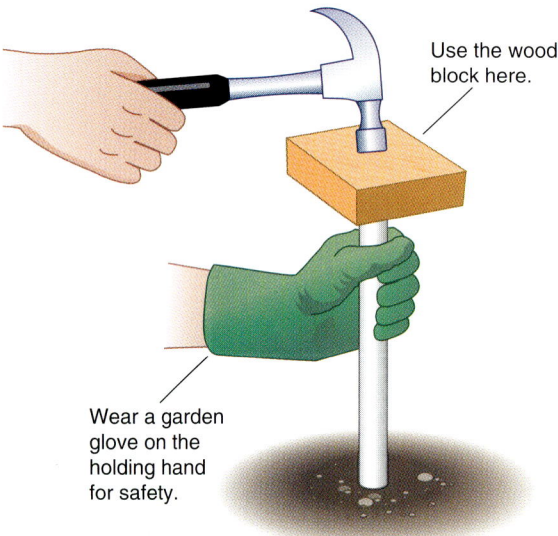

Use the wood block here.

Wear a garden glove on the holding hand for safety.

1. Stick the sharp end of a PVC pipe into the ground. Set a wooden block on top. Be sure to wear a garden or work glove on the hand holding the pipe.

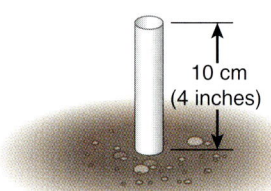

10 cm (4 inches)

2. Hammer the pipe into the ground leaving 10 cm (4") sticking above the surface.

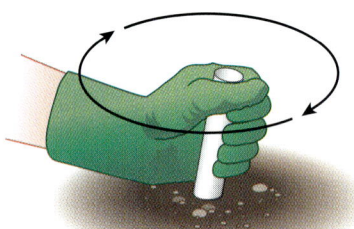

3. Grasp and move the pipe gently in a circular motion to loosen it from the ground. If the pipe is stuck, use gentle side-taps with the hammer to free it. Carefully pull the pipe out of the ground. If the soil does not remain inside the pipe, repeat the procedure somewhere else nearby.

Use caution in traveling to the site.

Collect only in areas where you have permission.

Investigation 4: Examining Core Samples of Soil

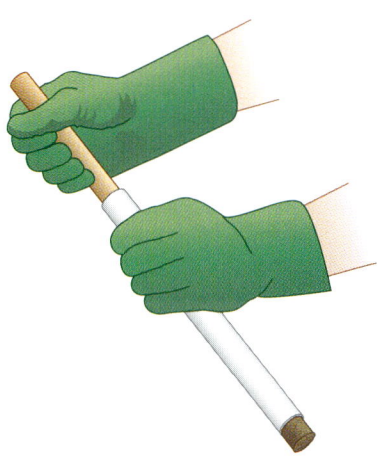

④ Insert a dowel into the open end of the pipe. Carefully push the core of soil out onto a flat surface covered with a sheet of plastic wrap.

⑤ If the soil core is very firm, gently tap the dowel with the hammer to release it. Make sure that the soil core stays together as much as possible.

⑥ Carefully wrap the core in the plastic wrap. If you roll the core up in several layers of the plastic wrap, it is more likely to stay intact while you carry it back to the classroom.

2. On a map of the sampling area, record the exact location where the soil sample was taken.

Collect soil samples with adult supervision only.

If living organisms are present inform your teacher.

Investigating Earth Systems

S
19

INVESTIGATING SOIL

Part 2: Analyzing the Soil Core Samples

1. Prepare your area in the classroom to analyze the soil core samples.

    Select the materials you will need.
    Spread a sheet of poster board on your table area.

2. Lay the core on the poster board, and unwrap it without breaking it. Observe it carefully.

    Using just your eyes, note any differences in the core from the top to the bottom. Look for color changes, different types of material, and any living things.

    a) Record any interesting things you observe.

    b) On the poster board, next to the core, draw a picture of the core. Use colored pencils to make the drawing as realistic as possible. Label the parts of the core you observed.

3. Use a plastic knife to make a long cut down the center of the core. Look at the inside.

    a) Record any interesting materials or items you uncover. Add them to your diagram.

4. Let the core dry out thoroughly.

    Gently break any lumps of soil with your thumb.

    With the plastic knife, spread the core material apart sideways until it is about 5 cm wide. Now you can study the materials in the core in more detail.

Break lumps of soil gently or, if they are too hard, discard them. Clean up spills immediately.

Investigation 4: Examining Core Samples of Soil

5. Use a hand lens to observe the different kinds of materials. Use the knowledge you gained in the last investigation to help you identify the materials.

   a) Record your observations. A data table like the one shown below can be helpful. You can make up your own table and use categories to suit your sample.

Material group	Type of material(s)	Color(s) of materials	Particle size	Name of material
1	stones	red/yellow	pea size	rock chips
2				
3				
4				
5				

6. In your group, examine your data.

   Consider and discuss the following questions:
   - Which materials in your core sample contain living (or once living) things? Which materials in your core sample have probably not come from living things? How can you tell? Which materials are you uncertain about?
   - Which materials tend to be near the top of the soil sample? Which tend to be near the bottom?
   - Which materials seem to be all through the core sample?
   - How could measurements help you to describe your sample?
   - What could you do to make measurements of the samples?

   a) Record any further data you uncovered in your discussion.

Investigating Earth Systems

INVESTIGATING SOIL

Inquiry

Studying Patterns and Relationships

Finding your own evidence does not always provide a complete explanation to a scientific question. Scientists look for evidence other scientists have collected. They then look for explanations by studying patterns and relationships within the evidence.

7. To make a soil map of your sampling area, you will need to present your findings and compare them to the findings of other groups in your class.

   Mark the location of each soil sample on one map of the area.

   Look for patterns and relationships between the soil samples and the areas where they were found. Consider the following:

   • What plants and animals are found at each location?
   • Is the location mostly high ground or mostly low ground?
   • What evidence of water is there? Is the area dry, moist, or wet?

   a) Think about similarities and differences among the soil samples. Try to group similar soil samples together on your map. Look for patterns of soil types, and record any patterns you find.

Part 3: Extending the Investigation

1. Your map will probably not be as complete as you would like. There may be places where you do not have enough data. There may be samples that raise further questions to investigate.

   Discuss what additional evidence you need to obtain to improve your soil map. Think about other questions you would like to investigate.

   a) Record questions you would like to investigate.

2. Using these questions, put together a reasonable plan for gathering the information you need.

   a) Record your plan for further investigation.

3. With the approval of your teacher, carry out your investigation.

Have your plan approved by your teacher before you begin.

Investigation 4: Examining Core Samples of Soil

Part 4: Using Other Resources

1. If possible, obtain professionally produced maps to provide you with additional information.

   Use print and electronic resources to gather additional information about soil and soil types.

   Consult a local gardening expert or civil engineer to obtain information about your local soil.

   a) Record any additional information you gather. Be sure to include the source from which you obtained the information.

Digging Deeper

Topographic Maps

There are many kinds of maps. Almost all of the U.S. is covered by topographic maps. Topographic maps show you land elevations such as hills and valleys. The hills and valleys are marked with a series of curves called contour lines. A contour line connects all the points on the land surface that are at the same elevation.

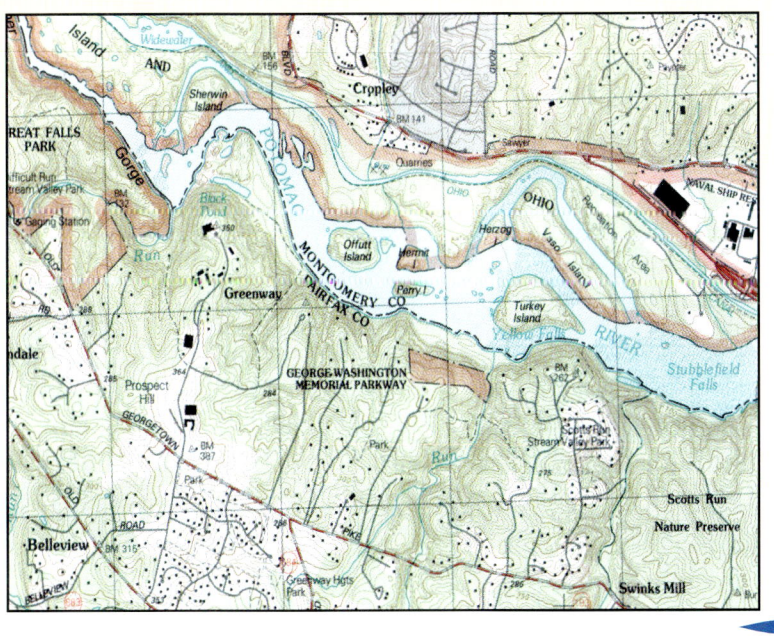

*As You Read...
Think about:
What does a topographic map show you?*

Investigating Earth Systems

INVESTIGATING SOIL

You can use a topographic map to see where streams and rivers flow. The area of the land that drains into a particular stream is called the watershed of that stream. Soil types usually differ quite a lot depending on where they are located in the watershed. Soils near the stream or river are usually thicker and better developed than soil in highlands.

You can also tell from a topographic map how steep the slope of the land is. The soil type often depends on the slope of the land. Soils on gently sloping land are usually thicker and better developed than soils on steep slopes.

In many areas of the United States, soil scientists have made soil maps, which show where different soil types are located at the Earth's surface. Your map is just this kind of soil map! If you can obtain a published soil map of your area, you can compare your map with the published map.

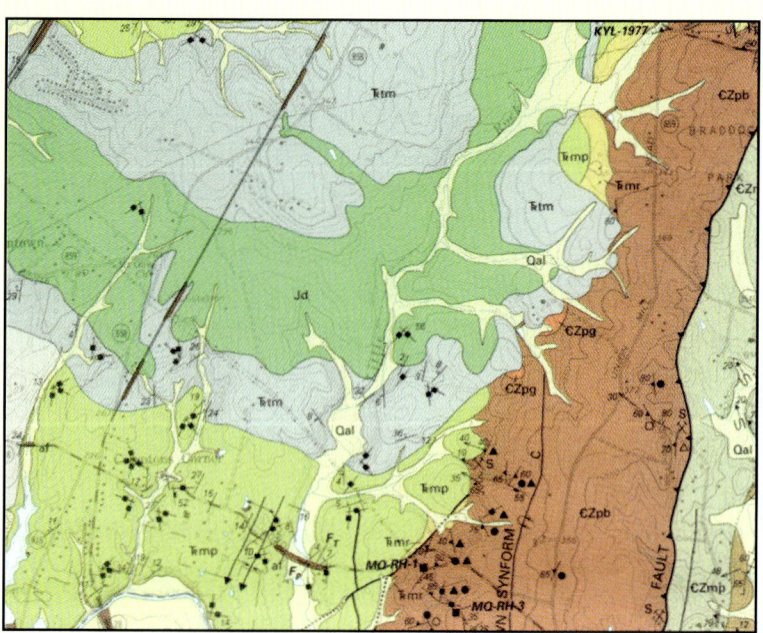

Investigation 4: Examining Core Samples of Soil

Review and Reflect

Review

1. What questions about soil has this investigation answered?
2. What characteristics of soil did you use to separate your soil samples?
3. What evidence did you use to identify living and non-living components of your soil sample?
4. How could you find out if two soil samples might have been taken from the same location?

Reflect

5. What have you learned about soil by comparing soil samples taken from different areas?
6. Based on what you now know, what new questions about soil do you think would be useful to investigate?

Thinking about the Earth System

7. Write any new connections that you have made between soil and the Earth system on your *Earth System Connections* sheet for soil.

Thinking about Scientific Inquiry

8. How did you use tools to collect data in this investigation?
9. In this investigation, why was it important for all groups to display their findings using the sample procedure?

INVESTIGATING SOIL

Investigation 5:

Water and Other Chemicals in Soil

Materials Needed

For this investigation your group will need:

- garden shovel
- watering can
- supply of water
- 4 clear-plastic (10 oz.) cups with small hole in bottom
- 4 clear-plastic (6 oz.) cups
- cup of sand
- cup of gravel
- cup of clay
- 2 large soup cans with ends removed
- wooden block
- hammer
- garden or work glove
- timing device
- soil-testing kit

Key Question

Before you begin, first think about this key question.

What chemicals are in soil?

By now you know that soil contains materials that come from both living and non-living things. These are the particles, big and small, that are fairly easy to see. Think about what other things, that are not so easy to see, might be in soil. Share your thinking with others in your group and with your class.

Investigate

Part 1: Observing a Soil Profile

1. As a class, go outside to the site that has been selected for you.

Investigation 5: Water and Other Chemicals in Soil

Dig into the soil with a shovel and expose the soil to a depth of about 45 cm (18").

Observe how the soil characteristics change the deeper you dig.

If possible, dig out a 30-cm (1') cube of soil to transport back to your classroom as an exhibit.

a) Use the soil profile shown in the diagram as a guide for making a sketch of the soil you have exposed. (The diagram represents a profile of soil that is old and has not been disturbed.)

2. Predict what you think will happen if you sprinkle a can full of water over the top of the soil you have exposed.

a) Record your prediction and the reason for your prediction.

3. Gently pour all the water from a full watering can over the soil. Make it as much like rain falling as possible.

a) Where does the water seem to go in the soil?

b) How can you tell that the water is moving through the soil?

c) Were your predictions and your reasoning accurate? If not, how can you explain any differences?

4. Repair the site where you exposed the soil.

Take your sketches and observation notes back with you to the classroom.

⚠️ Use caution when using the shovel. After use, place it where it will not be stepped on or tripped over.

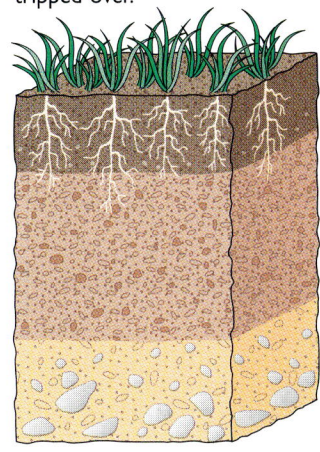

⚠️ When repairing the site, be sure that the hole will not be a hazard for passers-by.

⚠️ Only dig in approved areas with permission of the landowner.

Investigating Earth Systems

S 27

INVESTIGATING SOIL

Inquiry
Measurement in Scientific Inquiry

Scientists use measurement in their investigations. Accurate measurement, with suitable units, is important for both collecting and analyzing data. Data often consist of numbers.

Part 2: Designing and Conducting Your Own Investigation

1. Think about how water passes through the spaces between soil particles, as well as the different materials in soil and their sizes.
   Set up the testing equipment as shown. Use one set for each different test material.

   You will test:
   - plant material;
   - sand;
   - gravel;
   - clay.

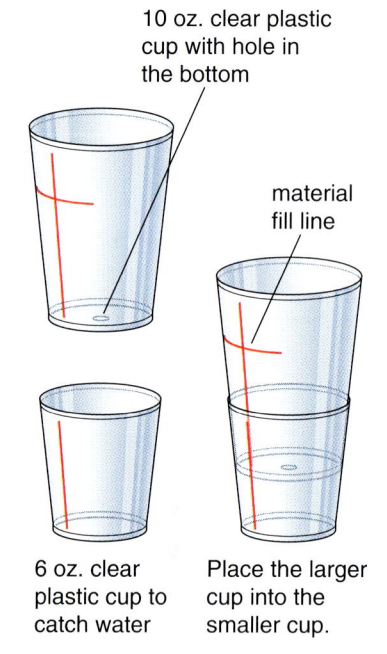

   10 oz. clear plastic cup with hole in the bottom

   material fill line

   6 oz. clear plastic cup to catch water

   Place the larger cup into the smaller cup.

2. In your group discuss how you could use the equipment and materials to develop a fair test.

   Your testing procedure should have:
   - a question to investigate;
   - a fair design;
   - a form of measurement that all can agree upon;
   - a clear method of recording observations and results;
   - a method that can be repeated to verify the results.

   a) Write down your procedure.

3. With the approval of your teacher, carry out your fair test.
   a) Record your data.

⚠ Have your plan approved by your teacher before you begin your investigation.

Investigation 5: Water and Other Chemicals in Soil

4. Share your findings with other groups in your class. Use everyone's results to answer the following questions:

   a) Which material lets water pass through it most quickly?

   b) How does the rate at which water passes through a material relate to the size of the particles in the material?

Part 3: Conducting a Percolation Test

1. Scientists use the term percolation to describe water passing through materials.

   Follow these steps to conduct a percolation test.

   1 Obtain a large soup can that has both ends removed.

   Mark a spot halfway up on the side of the can.

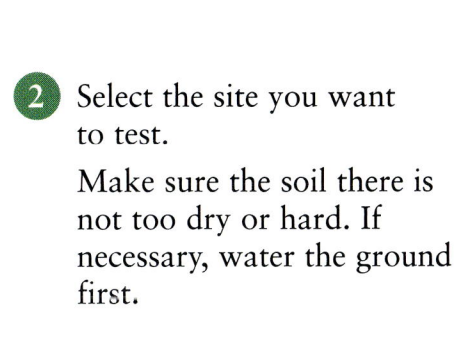

   Mark the halfway spot on the empty soup can.

   2 Select the site you want to test.

   Make sure the soil there is not too dry or hard. If necessary, water the ground first.

Clean up any spills immediately.

Inquiry

Following Standard Procedures

You are going to run a percolation test on soil. This test is similar to the one professionals use in the field to find the rate at which water moves through soil. You want to be able to compare your results with others. Therefore, it is important that all tests be done using exactly the same procedure.

Investigating Earth Systems

S 29

INVESTIGATING SOIL

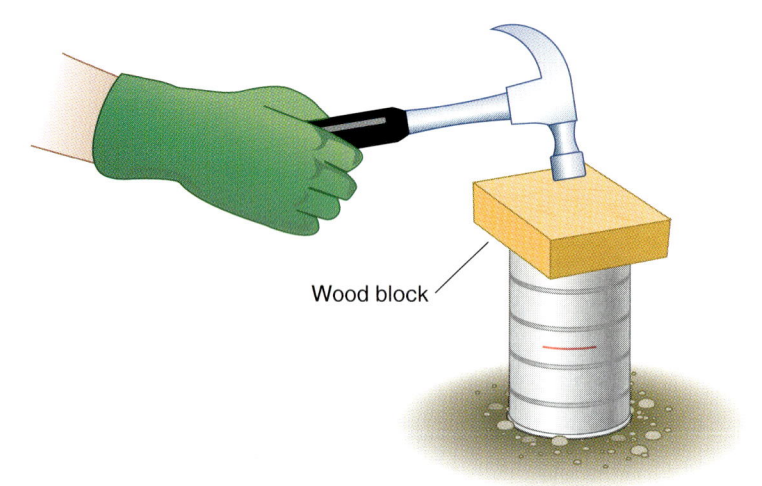

3 Set the can vertically into the ground.

Place a wooden block on the can.

Hammer the block so that it pushes the can about halfway into the ground.

Wood block

4 Fill the can above the soil with water.

Time how long it takes for the water to drain from the can into the soil below.

⚠ Conduct the percolation test under adult supervision only.

⚠ Use all necessary precautions when examining your soil sample.

2. Collect and review the data.

   a) Record your data.

   b) From your data, predict what type of soil particles are likely to be found where you ran your percolation test.

   c) Compare your data with others in the class to build a picture of the area you tested.

3. Take a core sample from the spot you tested.

   Examine the sample.

   a) Was your prediction of the type of soil particles correct? Explain any differences.

Investigation 5: Water and Other Chemicals in Soil

Part 4: Testing for Other Chemicals

1. Obtain a soil-testing kit. Examine the kit carefully. Read to find out:
   - what different chemicals the kit measures;
   - why these chemicals are important in the soil;
   - what testing procedures have to be followed;
   - any safety precautions that should be observed.

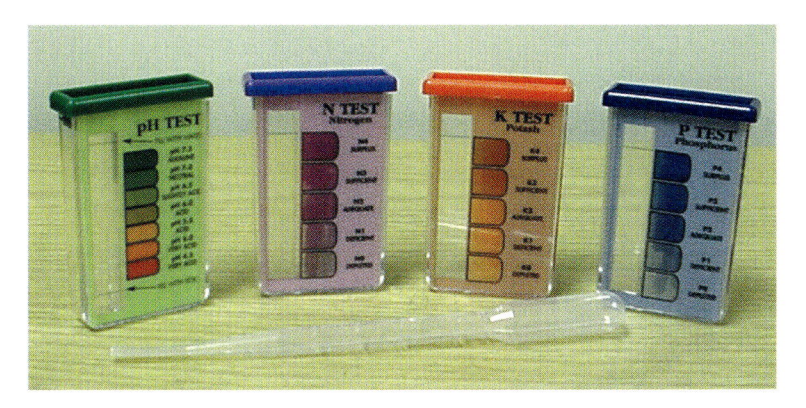

   Materials in soil-test kits can be harmful if swallowed. Be sure you understand all safety precautions and handle the chemicals responsibly.

2. Run the tests as directed on the kit. Remember, it is always a good idea to repeat your tests several times to get reliable results.

   a) Record your results in a form that others can see and understand.

3. In your group analyze your results.

   a) What chemicals are at a high level in your sample? What chemicals are at a low level?

   b) Combine these results with what you found out earlier about water, solid particles, plant life, and other aspects of your soil samples. This information will be very useful in (the final) Investigation 7.

   c) Pool all the data collected by the class. Add all new items to your soil maps.

Investigating Earth Systems

S 31

INVESTIGATING SOIL

As You Read...
Think about:
1. Why is it important to know the drainage rate of soil?
2. Why are water and other chemicals in soil important?
3. What is pH level and why is it important to plants?
4. What chemicals are important to plant growth?

Digging Deeper

The Importance of Water and Other Chemicals in Soil

Knowing how water passes through soil is very important. For example, engineers need to know how quickly water will drain away from buildings or bridges. Drainage rates are also important to farmers, landscapers, gardeners, environmental scientists, and other professionals.

Water is one chemical found in soil. There are many others. Some of the chemicals in soil are very important for plant growth. Farmers and gardeners often test their soil for these chemicals. They use soil-testing kits. These kits can be bought at gardening or hardware stores.

Investigation 5: Water and Other Chemicals in Soil

Soil-testing kits can test to see how acidic or basic a soil is. (Vinegar is acidic, and many soaps are basic.) The measure for how much acid or base there is in soil is called the pH level. A pH of 7 means that there is no more acid than base present. The solution is neutral. Lower numbers indicate acids. Higher numbers indicate the presence of bases. The pH controls how well plants use the food (nutrients) available in the soil. Different plants prefer different pH levels. The testing kit you use may tell you which plants do better at a given pH. The pH level in soil can be changed by adding chemicals.

Three chemicals are very important for plants. They are:
- nitrogen that affects the growth of leaves;
- phosphorus that helps roots grow strong;
- potassium that helps flowers and fruits grow.

Soil-testing kits can tell you how much of each chemical there is in a soil sample. Different plants need different amounts of these chemicals. Lawn grasses need a high level of nitrogen. Fruits need less nitrogen but higher levels of phosphorus and potassium. Root vegetables need lower levels of nitrogen and potassium and much higher levels of phosphorus.

Investigating Earth Systems

INVESTIGATING SOIL

Review and Reflect

Review

1. Look again at the key question. Has the investigation helped you answer the question? Based on your investigation, what chemicals are in your soil sample?

2. Suppose you were to conduct percolation tests on soil that contained a lot of clay and soil that contained a lot of gravel. Which would you predict would take less time?

3. Based on the result of your investigation and your reading, explain why it is important to know what chemicals are in soil.

Reflect

4. Where do you think the chemicals in soil come from?

5. How could you use what you know about soil in a practical way?

6. Based on what you now know, what further questions about chemicals in soil would be useful to investigate?

Thinking about the Earth System

7. How do water and other chemicals in soil connect to the geosphere, hydrosphere, atmosphere, and biosphere? Include any new connections on your *Earth System Connections* sheet for soil.

Thinking about Scientific Inquiry

8. Describe how you used evidence to develop ideas in this investigation.

9. Why was it important for everyone to follow the same procedure exactly when doing the percolation test?

10. Explain where you used measurement and why it was important in this investigation.

Investigation 6: Soil Erosion

Investigation 6:
Soil Erosion

Key Question

Before you begin, first think about this key question.

How is soil worn away?

Think about what you already know about how soil is formed. What factors could act on soil to make it wear away? Share your thinking with others in your group and with your class.

Materials Needed:

For this investigation your group will need:

- stream table or large plastic tray with end cut open
- soil sample to fill the tray
- tube or hose connected to a water faucet
- large garbage pail
- small piece of wood or other item to prop up tray
- large sponge
- large sample of dry soil, about 5 kg (10 lb.)
- electric window fan, or a fan on a stand
- plastic drop cloth
- dust masks

Investigate

Part 1: Soil Erosion by Running Water

1. Set the stream table on a table top with the open end hanging over the edge.
   Place the pail under the open end of the tray at the edge of the table. Fill the tray with the soil sample to a depth of about 2 to 3 cm (1").

Investigating Earth Systems

S 35

INVESTIGATING SOIL

Inquiry
Using Models in Scientific Inquiry

Scientists often use models as a way of studying and explaining things that cannot be observed directly. Modeling can also simulate processes that take a very long time in the real world. You will use a stream table to model soil erosion.

Explorations

Not all experiments are as well planned as the ones you have been conducting in the previous investigations. Sometimes, scientists do experiments just to watch and think. They then develop ideas for further experiments. This is a kind of exploration. Exploration is an important part of scientific inquiry. The experiments you are doing in this investigation are explorations.

⚠️ Arrange the stream table so that water flow can be stopped easily in case it begins to overflow. Clean spills immediately.

Level the surface of the soil and pack it down gently.

Raise the closed end of the tray by putting the small piece of wood under it.

Put the sponge on the soil surface at the upper end of the tray.

2. The idea is to explore what flowing water does to the soil. To do this, hold the end of the hose a short distance above the sponge and very gradually increase the flow of water. The purpose of the sponge is to break the force of the water jet that comes from the hose.

   Watch the soil surface in the tray carefully until some of the soil particles are moved by the flow of water.

   a) Take written notes, in as much detail as you can, about how the soil particles are moved by the water.

3. Increase the water flow slightly, and make more observations.

   Continue increasing the flow and making observations.

   a) Record all your observations.

4. Use your observations to answer the following questions:

   a) How did the movement of the coarser soil particles differ from the movement of the finer soil particles?

   b) Is the soil erosion concentrated in one place, or does it affect the whole width of the tray?

   c) Are some of the soil particles too large or too heavy to be moved by even a strong water flow?

Investigating Earth Systems

Investigation 6: Soil Erosion

5. In your small groups discuss further investigations you would like to do based on your exploration. For example, you may study ways to prevent or lessen the erosion of the soil by the flowing water.

   Share your ideas with the class.

   Design an investigation to test if your predictions were correct.

   a) List the materials you will need, the steps of the investigation, and your prediction. Don't forget to give a reason for your prediction.

   b) With the approval of your teacher carry out your investigation. Record your findings. Were your predictions correct?

Part 2: Soil Erosion by Wind

1. As a class, go outside to an open area on a nice day with little wind.

   Spread the drop cloth out on the open area. Weigh the corners down with bricks or heavy books.

   About one-third of the way in from one edge of the drop cloth, spread a patch of the soil sample about 1 cm thick. The soil should cover an area about 60 cm (2') on a side.

   Place the fan on the drop cloth about 1 m (3') away from the edge of the patch of soil.

   Aim the fan across the soil sample and toward the center of the drop cloth. Direct the fan slightly downward toward the soil.

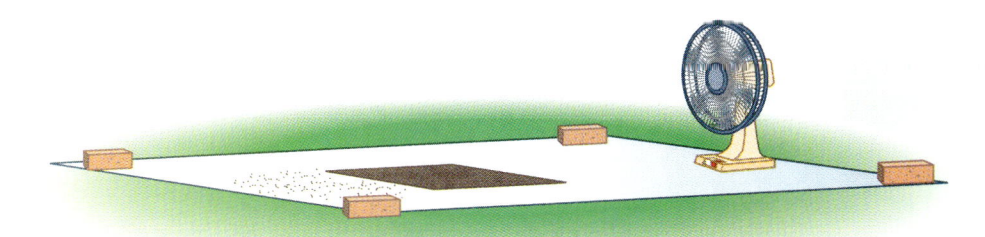

Investigating Earth Systems

INVESTIGATING SOIL

⚠ Blowing dust can cause eye irritation. Stay away from where the soil is blowing. Use eye and mouth protection.

2. Put on safety goggles and a dust mask.

   Turn the fan on to a low speed. If the fan is far enough away from the soil, none of the soil particles will be moved by the fan.

   Increase the speed of the fan to medium or high speed. If some of the soil particles are moved, observe carefully how they are moved.

   a) Record your observations.

3. Turn the fan off, and slide it a bit closer to the soil.

   Turn the fan on again, and observe the movement of the soil.

   Keep moving the fan closer to the soil to model a stronger and stronger wind.

   a) Carefully, with as much detail as possible, record your observations.

4. Use your observations to answer the following questions:

   a) How does the motion of the soil particles in the wind differ from the motion of the soil particles in the water flow? How is it similar?

   b) How does the movement of the coarser soil particles differ from the movement of the finer soil particles?

   c) Are some of the soil particles too large or too heavy to be moved by even a strong flow of air?

   d) How far do you think the finest soil particles might travel in the wind?

5. In your small groups discuss further investigations you would like to do based on your exploration. For example, you may study how compacting the soil, or watering the soil might affect the amount of erosion by the wind.

   Share your ideas with the class.

   Design an investigation to test if your predictions were correct.

   a) Record materials you will need, the steps of the investigation, and your prediction. Don't forget to give a reason for your prediction.

   b) With the approval of your teacher carry out your investigation. Record your findings. Were your predictions correct?

⚠ Have your plan approved by your teacher before you begin your investigation.

Investigation 6: Soil Erosion

Digging Deeper

Soil Erosion

Water or air that moves over a soil surface applies forces to the soil particles on the surface. If the forces are large enough, they move the particles. The stronger the current or wind, the more particles are put into motion. Larger and heavier particles tend to roll or hop near the soil surface. Finer and lighter particles are carried upward from the soil surface. In nature, the finest particles may be carried for hundreds or even thousands of kilometers high in the atmosphere before they fall out!

Soil erosion is a serious problem in many areas of the world. Soil takes thousands of years to form, but much of it can be eroded by just a few unusually heavy rainstorms or strong winds.

Bare soil surfaces are very likely to be eroded by a sudden heavy rainstorm. The running water can cut a channel, called a gully, in the soil surface. Once the gully is cut, the force of the water is focused there. This deepens the channel.

Investigating Earth Systems

INVESTIGATING SOIL

One very good way to reduce soil erosion is to keep the soil surface covered with vegetation. Another way is to plant crops in rows that follow the contours of the land surface rather than running up and down a slope.

Investigation 6: Soil Erosion

Review and Reflect

Review

1. Look again at the key question. Has the investigation helped you answer the question? Based on your investigation, how is soil worn away?

2. Suppose you were to conduct this investigation on soil that contained a lot of gravel and soil that contained fine sand. Which would you predict would erode more quickly?

3. Based on the result of your investigation and your reading, explain why soil erosion is important.

Reflect

4. Where do you think the soil that is eroded goes?

5. How could you use what you found out in this investigation in a practical way?

6. Based on what you now know, what further questions about soil erosion would be useful to investigate?

Thinking about the Earth System

7. How is water (hydrosphere) involved in soil erosion?

8. How is air (atmosphere) involved in soil erosion?

9. How could the biosphere be involved in soil erosion?

10. How does soil erosion connect to the geosphere, hydrosphere, atmosphere, and biosphere? Include any new connections on your *Earth System Connections* sheet for soil.

Thinking about Scientific Inquiry

11. How did you use models to help you study soil erosion?

12. Could you observe soil erosion without using models? If so, where would you go to make your observations?

13. What are the advantages and disadvantages of using models?

INVESTIGATING SOIL

Investigation 7:

Using Soil Data to Plan a Garden

Key Question
Before you begin, first think about this key question.

What soil mixtures are best for plants?

In this last investigation you will have a chance to apply all that you have learned about soil to solve a practical problem. You are going to plan a garden for your school grounds, or your local area. Think about all the things that you have learned about soil that you will need to answer the key question.
Share your ideas with others in your class.

Materials Needed
For this investigation your group will decide what materials are needed.

Consider all necessary safety precautions at every phase of planning and carrying out the project.

Investigate

1. Choose an area on your school grounds or in your community where you think you might want to plant a garden.

    Obtain permission to use the site for planning the garden.

Investigation 7: Using Soil Data to Plan a Garden

2. When you have permission to use the site for planning, obtain some soil samples from the area.

3. Divide the work of analyzing the samples among the different groups in the class. Look over all the previous investigations you have done. Decide how your group will analyze the samples. Review the method you will use.

   a) In your notebook list the materials you will need. Record the method you will use for your analysis.

4. Run your tests.

   a) Record all your data.

   b) As a class, combine your results. You may wish to use a data table similar to the one shown. Change it to suit your needs. It may be helpful to use a separate table for each sample.

Soil Analysis Data Table for Soil Sample			
Soil Analysis	Test 1	Test 2	Test 3
Observational data			
Soil components			
Water content			
Water drainage			
pH level			
Phosphorus level			
Nitrogen level			
Potassium level			
Other aspects			

Investigating Earth Systems

INVESTIGATING SOIL

5. Use the completed data table and any gardening resources to decide which plants will do well in your area. Consider how you will balance the following factors:
   - the soil type;
   - plants that grow well in that soil type;
   - plants that you would like to grow;
   - ways in which you could change your soil without harming the environment and without costing a lot;
   - the light available;
   - the climate in your area;
   - direction and steepness of the ground slope.

   a) Record the names of the plants you wish to grow. Note the growing conditions required for each plant.

   b) Make a detailed plan of your garden.

6. Try to arrange interviews with one or more experienced local gardeners. This is very important. You have planned carefully. However, these people may know things about your area that you may not have thought of.

   a) After listening to their advice, revise your plan if you think you need to.

Investigation 7: Using Soil Data to Plan a Garden

7. Share your plan with the rest of the class. Make sure that your garden plan, and all the information supporting it, is in a form that can be seen and understood by others.

   As a class, work towards one overall plan.

   Develop a presentation of your plan that you can use to convince the persons in charge to carry out your ideas. Here is an example of a plan to help you get started.

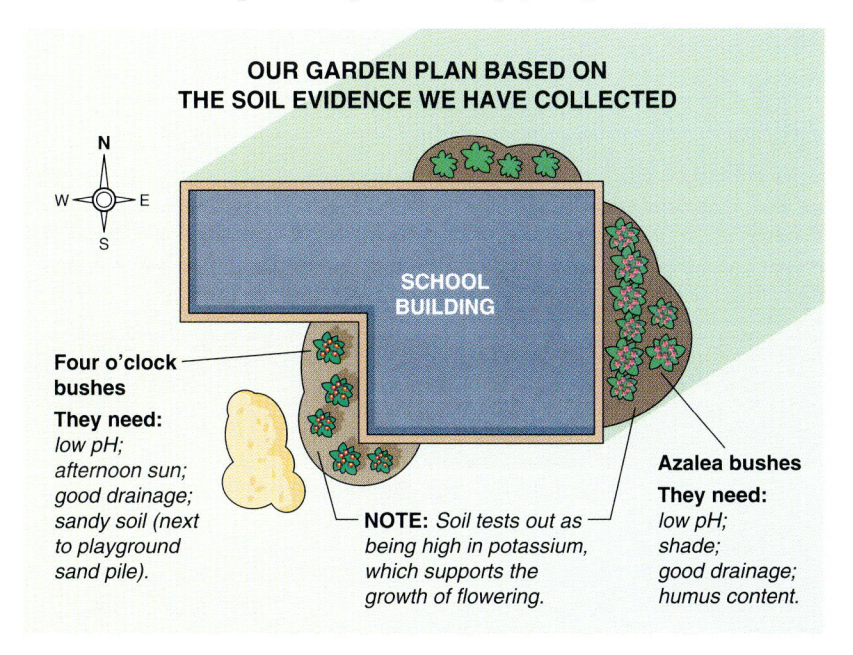

   OUR GARDEN PLAN BASED ON THE SOIL EVIDENCE WE HAVE COLLECTED

   Four o'clock bushes
   They need:
   low pH;
   afternoon sun;
   good drainage;
   sandy soil (next to playground sand pile).

   NOTE: Soil tests out as being high in potassium, which supports the growth of flowering.

   Azalea bushes
   They need:
   low pH;
   shade;
   good drainage;
   humus content.

8. To complete your plan, you will need to figure out costs. Check prices for:
   - the plants you plan to include;
   - any materials you need to add to the soil;
   - any other items you will need to carry out your plan.

   a) Record the costs needed to carry out your plan.

9. Present your plan. If possible, carry out your ideas.

Investigating Earth Systems

S 45

INVESTIGATING SOIL

Review and Reflect

Review

1. Were there any surprises in other groups' plans or evidence? If so, how can you explain them?
2. How was your plan the same and/or different from those of other groups?

Reflect

3. How has this investigation given you a better understanding of the relationship between soil and plants?
4. Why is the relationship between soil and plants important?
5. Why is it important to prevent soil erosion?

Thinking about the Earth System

6. How do plants and soil relate to the Earth Systems?

Thinking about Scientific Inquiry

7. Explain how you have applied the processes of scientific inquiry to solve a practical problem.

Reflecting

Back to the Beginning
You have been investigating soil in many ways. How have your ideas about soil changed from when you started? Look at the following questions and write down your ideas now.

- What is soil, and what is it made of?
- How is soil formed and how does it wear away?
- Why is soil important, and why is it important for you to know about soil?
- What questions do you have about soil?

How has your thinking about soil changed?

Thinking about the Earth System
At the end of each investigation, you thought about how your findings connected with the Earth system. Consider what you have learned about the Earth system. Refer to the *Earth System Connections* sheet that you have been building up throughout this module.

- What connections between soil and the Earth system have you been able to find?

Thinking about Scientific Inquiry
You have used inquiry processes throughout the module. Review the investigations you have done and the inquiry processes you have used.

- What scientific inquiry processes did you use?
- How did scientific inquiry processes help you learn about soil?

Not so much an ending, as a new beginning!

This investigation into soil is now completed. However, this is not the end of the story. You will see soil where you live, and everywhere you travel. Be alert for opportunities to observe soils and add to your understanding.

INVESTIGATING SOIL

The Big Picture

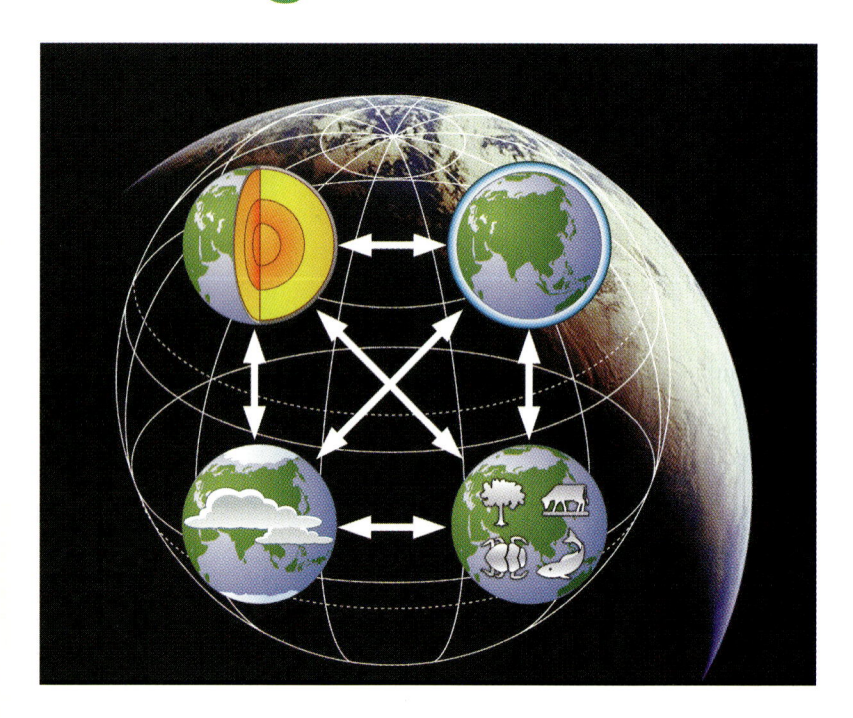

Key Concepts

Earth is a set of closely linked systems.

Earth's processes are powered by two sources: the Sun, and Earth's own inner heat.

The geology of Earth is dynamic, and has evolved over 4.5 billion years.

The geological evolution of Earth has left a record of its history that geoscientists interpret.

We depend upon Earth's resources—both mined and grown.

Glossary

Analyze - Consider data in terms of any patterns or relationships that emerge.

Atmosphere - The mixture of gases that surround the Earth.

Biological weathering - The processes of weathering by which living things, including animals, plants, and other organisms, break down rock into smaller pieces or particles, at, or near, the Earth's surface.

Biosphere - The part of the Earth System that includes all living things, including animals, plants, and other organisms.

Chemicals - Elements or compounds. The smallest part of an element that retains its characteristics is an atom. The smallest part of a compound that retains its characteristics is a molecule.

Chemical weathering - The processes of weathering by which chemical reactions break down and transform rocks and minerals into new chemical combinations at, or near, the Earth's surface.

Crust - The outermost layer of the Earth, composed of rock, representing less than 0.1% of the Earth's total volume.

Data - Data are the observations, both quantitative and qualitative, which result from an experiment.

Design - A plan for investigation. This could be a laboratory experiment, model, simulation, field study, or other type of investigation.

Deposition - The laying down of rock-forming material by any natural agent such as: the physical settling of sediment suspended in water; the chemical precipitation of mineral matter from solution.

Earth System - A term used to describe the Earth as a set of closely interacting Systems, including all sub-Systems such the geosphere, lithosphere, atmosphere, hydrosphere, biosphere, and others.

Erosion - The weathering away of soil or rock by weathering, and the action of streams, glaciers, waves, wind, and underground water.

Erosional landforms - A land surface shaped and subdued by the action of erosion.

Evidence - Data which supports a scientific conclusion.

Experiment - A fair test of a hypothesis.

Experimenting - The process of conducting a fair test.

Fair test - A fair test is an experiment in which only one variable is tested at a time. A fair test also involves a control, a well-defined research question, collection and verification of data, and repeated trials.

Field work - Field work is testing done in a "real world" setting outside the laboratory. It can include sample collection, testing on-site, observations of nature, and many other aspects of non-laboratory science.

Findings - Experimental results or conclusions.

INVESTIGATING SOIL

Geology - The study of planet Earth - the materials of which it is made, the processes that act on these materials, the products formed, and the history of the planet and all its life forms since its origin.

Geologist - One who is trained in and works in any of the geological sciences.

Geologic map - A map on which is recorded the distribution, nature, and age relationships of rock units and the occurrence of structural features.

Geosphere - The part of the Earth System that includes the crust, mantle, and inner core.

Hydrosphere - The part of the Earth System that includes all the planet's water, including oceans, lakes, rivers, ground water, ice, and water vapor.

Inquiry - Inquiry is the process of finding answers to questions through a variety of methods. These can include research, fair testing, using models, asking experts, or many other methods.

Inquiry processes - Inquiry processes are the methods used by scientists to find answers to questions. They include hypothesizing, observing, recording, analyzing, concluding, communicating, and others.

Inquiry questions - Inquiry questions are those questions designed to be answered through a Systematic, scientific process.

Landform - One of the numerous features that taken together make up the surface of the Earth, including broad features such as plain, plateau, and mountain, and also minor features such as hill, valley, slope, canyon, flatland, wetland, delta, shoreline, island, and so on.

Layers of sediment - A succession of different layers of sedimentary material, oldest at the bottom through youngest at the top, each deposited in turn by the settling of sediment in water, or the precipitation of minerals from solution.

Liquids - Substances in the state of matter in which their molecules are not as far apart as gases, but are farther apart than solids.

Model - A model is a representation of a process, System, or object which is too big, too small, too unwieldy, or too unsafe to test directly.

Modeling - Modeling is the process by which a representation of a process, System, or object is used to investigate a scientific question.

Observations - Data collected through the five senses.

Observe - To observe is to use the five senses to collect information about an object, event, or System.

Percolate - To percolate is to drip through a particulate medium through the force of gravity.

Percolation - The process by which a liquid drips downward through particulate medium.

Percolation tests - Percolation tests measure the rate at which a liquid travels downward through a particulate medium.

Physical weathering - The processes of weathering by which rock is broken down by physical forces such as, gravity, water, ice, wind, or human actions at, or near, the Earth's surface.

Particle - A term used to describe a small and separate unit in a rock, such as fragment or grain.

Glossary

Prediction - A prediction is a reasonable estimate of the outcome of a scientific test. Predictions are based upon previous experiments and other research.

Pressure - Pressure is a pushing force. One unit of measuring pressure is in PSIs, or pounds per square inch.

Rate - The measure of distance over time.

Record - To make a note of observations and events. Recording can be done on paper, electronically or through other means of communication such as video, sound recording, or photography.

Relief - The physical configuration of a part of the Earth's surface, with reference to variations in height and slope or to irregularities of the land surface.

Research report - A record of the processes and result of an investigation.

Results - Findings from an investigation.

Rock - Solid material which is either a collection of one or more minerals, or a body of mixed mineral matter, or solid organic matter.

Rock abrasion - The mechanical wearing or grinding away of rock surfaces by the friction and impact of rock particles transported by wind, ice, waves, running water, or gravity.

Rock cycle - A sequence of events involving the formation, alteration, destruction, and reformation of rocks as the result of such processes as erosion, transportation, deposition, lithification, and metamorphism.

Sample - A small amount of a larger quantity of matter, usually taken to be observed or tested.

Scientific inquiry - The process of investigating scientific questions in a Systematic and reproducible manner.

Scientific processes - The methods used by scientists to investigate questions, record data, and analyze results.

Sediment - Solid material that has settled down from a state of suspension in a liquid.

Soil - The natural medium for the growth of land plants. All unconsolidated materials above bedrock

Soil map - A map showing the distribution of various soil types in an area or region.

Topographic map - A map showing the topographic features of a land surface, commonly using contour lines.

Topography - The general configuration of a land surface including its relief and the position of its natural and human-made features.

Transportation - The movement of sediment by natural agents such as flowing water, ice, wind, or gravity, either in solid particles or in solution, from one place to another on the Earth's surface.

Variables - Variables are those parts of an experiment that can be changed. In a fair test, only one variable is changed at a time.

Verify - To check data for its reliability.

Water - A pure substance consisting of molecules of two hydrogen atoms bonded to one atom of oxygen.

Watershed - A drainage basin. The direction in which water drains from land.

Watershed map - A map showing the route taken by water draining from land

Weathering - The destructive processes by which rocks are changed on exposure to atmospheric agents at or near the Earth's surface.

INVESTIGATING SOIL

The American Geological Institute and Investigating Earth Systems

Imagine more than 300,000 Earth scientists worldwide sharing a common voice, and you've just imagined the mission of the American Geological Institute. Our mission is to raise public awareness of the Earth sciences and the role that they play in mankind's use of natural resources, mitigation of natural hazards, and stewardship of the environment. For more than 50 years, AGI has served the scientists and teachers of its Member Societies and hundreds of associated colleges, universities, and corporations by producing Earth science educational materials, *Geotimes*–a geoscience news magazine, GeoRef–a reference database, and government affairs and public awareness programs.

So many important decisions made every day that affect our lives depend upon an understanding of how our Earth works. That's why AGI created *Investigating Earth Systems*. In your *Investigating Earth Systems* classroom, you'll discover the wonder and importance of Earth science. As you investigate minerals, soil, or oceans — do field work in nearby beaches, parks, or streams, explore how fossils form, understand where your energy resources come from, or find out how to forecast weather — you'll gain a better understanding of Earth science and its importance in your life.

We would like to thank the AGI Foundation Members that have been supportive in bringing Earth science to students. These AGI Foundation Members include: Anadarko Petroleum Corp., Baker Hughes Foundation, Barrett Resources Corp., BPAmoco Foundation, Burlington Resources Foundation, Chevron Foundation, Conoco Inc., Consolidated Natural Gas Foundation, Diamond Offshore Co., EEX Corp., ExxonMobil Foundation, Global Marine Drilling Co., Halliburton Foundation, Inc., Kerr McGee Foundation, Maxus Energy Corp., Noble Drilling Corp., Occidental Petroleum Charitable Foundation, Parker Drilling Co., Phillips Petroleum Co., Santa Fe Snyder Corp., Schlumberger Foundation, Shell Oil Company Foundation, Southwestern Energy Co., Texaco, Inc., Texas Crude Energy, Inc., Unocal Corp. USX Foundation (Marathon Oil Co.).

We at AGI wish you success in your exploration of the Earth System!

Michael J. Smith
Director of Education, AGI

Marcus E. Milling
Executive Director, AGI